Theories About Reincarnation and Spirits

By Helena P. Blavatsky

Copyright © 2021 Lamp of Trismegistus. All rights reserved. No part of this publication may be reproduced or transmitted in any form or by any means, electronic or mechanical, including photocopying, recording, or by any information storage and retrieval system, without permission in writing from Lamp of Trismegistus. Reviewers may quote brief passages.

ISBN: 978-1-63118-590-8

Esoteric Classics

Other Books in this Series and Related Titles

The Hymns of Hermes by G R S Mead (978-1-63118-405-5)

Clairvoyance and Psychic Abilities by A Besant &c (978-1-63118-403-1)

Gnosis of the Mind by G R S Mead (978-1-63118-408-6)

Rosicrucian Rules, Secret Signs, Codes and Symbols by various (978-1-63118-488-8)

An Outline of Theosophy by C W Leadbeater (978-1-63118-452-9)

Paracelsus, the Four Elements and Their Spirits by M P Hall (978-1-63118-400-0)

Essays on Ancient Magic by Helena P Blavatsky (978-1-63118-535-9)

Essays on the Esoteric Tradition of Karma by A Besant &c (978-1-63118-426-0)

The Use of Evil by Annie Besant (978-1-63118-532-8)

Occult Arts by William Q. Judge (978-1-63118-559-5)

The Alchemical Catechism of Paracelsus by Paracelsus (978-1-63118-513-7)

Alchemy in the Nineteenth Century by Helena P Blavatsky (978-1-63118-446-8)

Qabbalistic Teachings and the Tree of Life by M P Hall (978-1-63118-482-6)

The Historic, Mythic and Mystic Christ by Annie Besant (978-1-63118-533-5)

The Hidden Mysteries of Christianity by Annie Besant (978-1-63118-534-2)

The Brotherhood of Religions by Annie Besant (978-1-63118-563-2)

The Religion of Theosophy by Bhagwan Das (978-1-63118-565-6)

Arcane Formulas or Mental Alchemy by W W Atkinson (978-1-63118-459-8)

The Machinery of the Mind by Dion Fortune (978-1-63118-451-2)

Vision of the Spirit by C. Jinarajadasa (978-1-63118-560-1)

The Leadbeater Reader: A Selection of Occult Essays (978-1-63118-483-3)

Audio versions are also available on Audible, Amazon and Apple

Other Books in this Series and Related Titles

The Use and Power of Thought by C W Leadbeater (978–1–63118–589–2)

Commentary on the Pymander by G R S Mead (978–1–63118–588–5)

Hypnotism and Mesmerism by Annie Besant (978–1–63118–587–8)

Spirits of Various Kinds by Helena P Blavatsky (978–1–63118–586–1)

The Hidden Language of Symbolism by Annie Besant (978–1–63118–585–4)

Eastern Magic & Western Spiritualism by Henry S Olcott (978–1–63118–584–7)

Spiritual Progress and Practical Occultism by H P Blavatsky (978–1–63118–583–0)

Memory and Consciousness by Besant & Blavatsky (978–1–63118–582–3)

The Origin of Evil by Helena P Blavatsky (978–1–63118–581–6)

The Camp of Philosophy: Studies in Alchemy by Bloomfield (978–1–63118–580–9)

The Testaments of the Twelve Patriarchs (978–1–63118–579–3)

Occult or Exact Science? by Helena P Blavatsky (978–1–63118–578–6)

Occultism, Semi-Occultism & Pseudo Occultism by A Besant (978–1–63118–577–9)

The Fourth-Gospel and Synoptical Problem by G R S Mead (978–1–63118–576–2)

On the Bhagavad-Gita by T Subba Row &c (978–1–63118–575–5)

What Theosophy Does for Us by C W Leadbeater (978–1–63118–574–8)

Spiritual Life for Man by Annie Besant (978–1–63118–573–1)

The Mysteries by Annie Besant (978–1–63118–572–4)

Fundamental Ideas of Theosophy by Bhagwan Das (978–1–63118–571–7)

Dreams: What They Are and Caused by C W Leadbeater (978–1–63118–570–0)

Communication Between Different Worlds by Annie Besant (978–1–63118–569–4)

Audio versions are also available on Audible, Amazon and Apple

Table of Contents

Introduction…7

Theories About Reincarnation and Spirits…9

On the Mysteries of Reincarnation…31

INTRODUCTION

The word "esoteric" can be difficult to define. Esotericism in general can be seen less as a system of beliefs and more as a category, which encompasses numerous, different systems of beliefs. It's a bit of juxtaposition, since the word "esoteric" indicates something that few people know about, while the term itself broadly covers numerous philosophies, practices, areas of study and belief systems.

In a greater sense, Esotericism acts as a storehouse for secret knowledge, which is often considered ancient (by *tradition, if not by fact),* passed down from generation to generation, in private. At various times in history, simply possessing the knowledge of some of these subjects, was considered illegal and a jailable offence, if discovered. This usually included such general topics as Alchemy, Pharmacology, Qabalah, Hermeticism, Occultism, Ceremonial Magic, Astrology, Divination, Rosicrucianism and so on. Collectively, these areas of study were often referred to as the esoteric sciences.

Sometimes, the outer garment of a subject isn't esoteric, while what is hidden beneath it, is. As an example, Freemasonry isn't necessarily esoteric by nature (at *least not anymore),* but certain signs, passwords and handshakes given to the candidate during their initiation, are in fact, esoteric, in the sense that they are hidden from the general public.

Today, in the twenty-first century, such topics are readily available at bookstores across the country, and numerous mainsteam publishers offer beginners guides and coffee-table volumes on many of these subjects, intended for mass appeal. Books like *"The Secret"* have turned previously arcane topics into household knowledge. All that being the case, however, it isn't to say that there still aren't buried secrets to uncover, ancient wisdom being ignored and forgotten mysteries to be explored. In fact, it is often that we are only able to further our own studies by standing on the shoulders of these disappearing giants.

Lamp of Trismegistus is doing its part to help preserve humanity's esoteric history by making some of these classics available to those students who are seeking to unearth the knowledge of these ancient colossi.

So, be sure to check other titles from our *Esoteric Classics* series, as well as our *Occult Fiction, Theosophical Classics, Foundations of Freemasonry Series, Supernatural Fiction, Paranormal Research Series, Studies in Buddhism* and our *Christian Apocrypha Series.* You can also download the audio versions of most of these titles from Amazon, Apple or Audible, for learning on the go.

THEORIES ABOUT REINCARNATION AND SPIRITS

Over and over again the abstruse and mooted question of Rebirth or Reincarnation has crept out during the first ten years of the Theosophical Society's existence. It has been alleged on *prima facie* evidence, that a notable discrepancy was found between statements made in *Isis Unveiled*, Volume I, pp. 351-2, and later teachings from the same pen and under the inspiration of the same Master.[See charge and answer, in *Theosophist*. August 1882]

In *Isis* it was held, reincarnation is denied. An occasional return, only of "depraved spirits" is allowed. ' Exclusive of that rare and doubtful possibility, *Isis* allows only three cases - abortion, very early death, and idiocy - in which reincarnation on this earth occurs." ("C. C. M." in *Light*, 1882.)

The charge was answered then and there as every one who will turn to the *Theosophist* of August, 1882, can see for himself. Nevertheless, the answer either failed to satisfy some readers or passed unnoticed. Leaving aside the strangeness of the assertion that *reincarnation* - i.e., the serial and periodical rebirth of every individual *monad* from *pralaya to pralaya* - [The cycle of existence during the manvantara - period before and after the beginning and completion of which every such "Monad" is absorbed and reabsorbed in the ONE soul, *anima mundi*.] is denied in the face of the fact that the doctrine is part and parcel and one of the fundamental features of Hinduism and Buddhism, the charge amounted virtually to this: the writer of the present, a professed admirer and student of Hindu philosophy, and as professed a follower of Buddhism years before *Isis* was written, by rejecting reincarnation must necessarily reject Karma likewise! For the latter is the very *corner* stone of Esoteric

9

philosophy and Eastern Religions; it is the grand and one pillar *on which hangs the whole philosophy of rebirths*, and once the latter is denied, the whole doctrine of Karma falls into meaningless verbiage.

Nevertheless, the opponents without stopping to think of the evident "discrepancy" between charge and fact, accused a Buddhist by profession of faith of denying reincarnation, hence also by implication - Karma. Adverse to wrangling with one who was a friend, and undesirous at the time, to enter upon a defence of details and internal evidence - a loss of time indeed - the writer answered merely with a few sentences. But it now becomes necessary to well define the doctrine. Other critics have taken the same line, and by misunderstanding the passages to that effect in Isis they have reached the same rather extraordinary conclusions.

To put an end to such useless controversies, it is proposed to explain the doctrine more clearly.

Although, in view of the later more minute renderings of the esoteric doctrines, it is quite immaterial what may have been written in *Isis* - an encyclopedia of occult subjects in which each of those is *hardly sketched* - let it be known at once, that the writer maintains the correctness of every word given out upon the subject in my earlier volumes. What was said in the *Theosophist* of August, 1882, may now be repeated here. The passage quoted from it may be, and is, most likely incomplete, chaotic, vague, perhaps clumsy, as are many more passages in that work, the first literary production of a foreigner who even now can hardly boast of her knowledge of the English language". Nevertheless it is quite correct so far as that collateral feature of reincarnation is therein concerned.

I will now give extracts from *Isis* and proceed to explain every passage criticized, wherein it was said that "a few *fragments* of this mysterious doctrine of reincarnation *as distinct from* metempsychosis" - would be then presented. Sentences now explained are in italics.

"Reincarnation, *i.e.*, the appearance of the same individual, or rather of his *astral monad, twice on the same planet* is not a rule in nature, it is an exception, like the teratological phenomenon of a two-headed infant. It is preceded by a *violation of the laws of harmony of nature*, and happens only when the latter *seeking* to *restore its disturbed equilibrium, violently throws back into earth-life the astral monad which had been tossed out of the circle of necessity by crime or accident.* Thus in cases of abortion, of infants dying before a certain age, and of congenital and incurable idiocy, nature's original design to produce a perfect human being, has been interrupted. Therefore, while the gross matter of each of those several entities is suffered to disperse itself at death, through the vast realm of being, *the immortal spirit and astral monad of the individual - the latter having been set apart to animate* a frame and the former to shed its divine light on the corporeal organization - *must try a second time to carry out the purpose of the creative intelligence.* (Volume I, page 351.)

Here the "astral monad" or body of the deceased personality - say of John or Thomas - is meant. It is that which, in the teachings of the Esoteric philosophy of Hinduism, is known under its name of *bhoot*; in the Greek philosophy is called the *simulacrum* or *umbra*, and in all other philosophies worthy of the name is said, as taught in the former, to disappear after a certain period more or less prolonged in *Kama-loka* - the Limbus of the Roman Catholic, or *Hades* of the Greeks.[Hades has surely never been meant for *Hell*. It was always the abode of the sorrowing shadows of astral bodies of the dead personalities. Western readers should remember Kama-loka is not karma-loka, for Kama means *desire*, and Karma does not.] It *is* "a violation of the laws of harmony of nature", though it be so decreed by those of *Karma* - every time that the astral monad, or the *simulacrum* of the personality - of John or Thomas - instead of running down to the end of its natural period of time in a body - finds itself (a) violently thrown out of it by whether early death or accident; or (b) is compelled in consequence of its unfinished task to re-appear, (*i.e., the same astral body wedded to the same immortal monad*) on earth again, in order to complete the unfinished task. Thus "it must try a second time to carry out the purpose of creative intelligence" or *law*".

"If reason has been so far developed as to become active and discriminative there is no [Had this word "immediate" been put at the time of publishing *Isis* between the two words "no" and "reincarnation" there would have been less room for dispute and controversy] *(immediate) reincarnation* on this earth, for the three parts of the triune man have been united together, and he is capable of running the race. But when the new being has not passed beyond the condition of Monad, or when, as in the idiot, the trinity has not been completed on earth and therefore cannot be so after death, the immortal spark which illuminates it, has to re-enter on the earthly plane as it was frustrated in its first attempt. Otherwise, the mortal or astral, and the immortal or divine souls, *could not progress in unison and pass onwards to the sphere above* [By "sphere above", of course "Devachan" was meant.] *(Devachan)*. Spirit follows a line parallel with that of matter; and the spiritual evolution goes hand in hand with the physical". The occult Doctrine teaches that

(1) There is no *immediate* reincarnation on Earth for the Monad, as falsely taught by the Reincarnationist Spiritists; nor is there any second incarnation at all for the *personal* or *false* Ego - *the perisprit* - save the exceptional cases mentioned. But that *(a)* there are rebirths or periodical reincarnations for the immortal Ego - " Ego" during the cycle of rebirths, and *non*-Ego, in Nirvana or Moksha when it becomes *impersonal* and *absolute*); for that Ego is the root of

every new incarnation, the string on which are threaded, one after the other, the false personalities or illusive bodies called men, in which the Monad-Ego incarnates itself during the cycle of births ; and (b) that such reincarnations take place not before 1,500, 2,000, and even 3,000 years of Devachanic life.

(2) That Manas - the seat of *Jiv*, that spark which runs the round of the cycle of birth and rebirths with the Monad, from the beginning to the end of a Manvantara - is the real *Ego*. That *(a)* the *Jiv* follows the divine monad that gives it spiritual life and immortality into Devachan - that therefore, it can neither be reborn before its appointed period, nor reappear on Earth *visibly* or *invisibly* in the *interim*; and *(b)* that, unless the fruition, the spiritual aroma of the Manas - or all these highest aspirations and spiritual qualities and attributes that constitute the higher *Self* of man become united to its monad, the latter becomes as *Non-* existent; since it is in esse "impersonal" and *per se* Egoless, so to say, and gets its spiritual colouring or flavour of Ego-tism only from each *Manas* during incarnation and after it is disembodied, and separated from all its lower principles.

(3) That the remaining four principles, or rather the 2-1/2 - as they are composed of the terrestrial portion of *Manas*, of its vehicle *Kama-Rupa* and *Linga Sarira* - the body dissolving immediately, and *prana* or the life principle along with it - that these principles having belonged to the *false* personality are unfit for Devachan. The latter is the state of Bliss, the reward for all the undeserved miseries of life,[The reader must bear in mind that the esoteric teaching maintains that save in cases of wickedness when man's nature attains the acme of Evil, and human terrestrial sin reaches *satanic* universal character, so to say, as *some Sorcerers do* - there is no punishment for the majority of mankind after death. The law of retribution as *Karma*, waits man at the threshold of his new

incarnation. Man is at host a wretched tool of evil, unceasingly forming new causes and circumstances. He is not always (if ever) responsible. Hence a period of rest and bliss in Devachan, with an utter temporary oblivion of all the miseries and sorrows of life. *Avitchi* is a *spiritual state* of the greatest misery and is only in store for those who have devoted *consciously* their lives to doing injury to others and have thus reached its highest spirituality of Evil.] and that which prompted man to sin, namely his terrestrial passionate nature can have no room in it.

Therefore the reincarnating principles are left behind in *Kama-loka*, firstly as a material residue, then later on as a reflection on the mirror of Astral light. Endowed with *illusive* action, to the day when having gradually faded out they disappear, what is it but the Greek Eidolon and the simulacrum of the Greek and Latin poets and classics?

"What reward or punishment can there be in that sphere of disembodied human entities for a foetus or a human embryo which had not even time to breathe on this earth, still less an opportunity to exercise the divine faculties of its spirit? Or, for an irresponsible infant, whose senseless monad remaining dormant within the astral and physical casket, could as little prevent him from burning himself as any other person to death? Or again for one idiotic from birth, the number of whose cerebral circumvolutions is only from twenty to thirty per cent, of those of sane persons, and who therefore is irresponsible for either his disposition, acts, or for the imperfections of his vagrant, half-developed intellect." (*Isis*, Volume I, page 352.)

These are then, the "exceptions" spoken of in *Isis*, and the doctrine is maintained now as it was then. Moreover, there is no "discrepancy" but only *incompleteness* - hence, misconceptions arising from later teachings. Then again, there are several important mistakes in *Isis* which, as the plates of the work had been *stereotyped* were not corrected in subsequent editions. -

One of such is on page 346, and another in connection with it and as a sequence on page 347.

The discrepancy between the first portion of the statement and the last, ought to have suggested the idea of an evident mistake. It is addressed to the spiritists, *reincarnationists* who take the more than ambiguous words of Apuleius as a passage that corroborates their claims for their "spirits" and reincarnation. Let the reader judge [Says Apuleius: "The soul is born in this world upon leaving the soul of the world (anima mundi) in which her existence precedes the one we all know (on earth). Thus, the Gods, who consider her proceedings in all the phases of various existences as a whole, punish her sometimes for sins committed during an *anterior life*. *She dies* when she separates herself from u body in which she crossed this life in a frail bark. And this is, if I mistake not, the secret meaning of the tumulary inscription, so simple for the initiate: *To the Gods manes who lived*. But this kind of death does not annihilate the soul, it only transforms (one portion of it) into a lemure. Lemures are the *manes*, or ghosts, which we know under the name *lares*. When they keep away and *show us a beneficent protection*, we honour in them the protecting divinities of the family hearth; but if their crimes sentence them to err, we call them *larvae*. They become a plague for the wicked, and the vain terror of the good". ("Du Dieu de Socrate" Apul class, pp. 143-145.)] whether Apuleius does not justify rather *our* assertions. We are charged with denying reincarnation and this is what we said there and then in *Isis*!

"The *philosophy* teaches that nature *never leaves her work unfinished; if baffled at the first attempt, she tries again*. When she evolves a human embryo, the intention is that a man shall be perfected - physically, intellectually, and spiritually. His body is to grow, mature, wear out, and die ; his mind unfold, ripen, and be harmoniously balanced; his divine spirit illuminate and blend easily with the inner man. No human being completes its grand cycle, or the "circle of necessity", until all these are accomplished. As the laggards in a race struggle and plod in their first quarter while the victor darts past the goal, so, in the race of immortality, some souls outspeed all the rest and reach the end, while their myriad competitors are toiling under the load of matter, close to the starting point. Some unfortunates fall out entirely and lose all chance of the prize; some retrace their steps and begin again".

Clear enough this, one should say. Nature baffled *tries again*. No one can pass out of this world, (our earth) without becoming perfected *physically, morally, and spiritually*. How can this be done, unless there is *a series of rebirths* required for the necessary perfection in each department - to evolute in the "circle of necessity", can surely never be found in one human life ? and yet this sentence is followed without any break by the following parenthetical statement: "This is what the Hindu dreads above all things - *transmigration* and *reincarnation* ; only on other and inferior planets, never on this one!!!

The last "sentence" is a fatal mistake and one to which the writer pleads *not guilty*. It is evidently the blunder of some "reader" who had no idea of Hindu philosophy and who was led into a subsequent mistake on the next page, wherein the unfortunate word "planet" is put for *cycle*. *Isis* was hardly, if ever, looked into after its publication by its writer, who had other work to do; otherwise there would have been an apology and a page pointing to the *errata* and the sentence made to run: "The Hindu dreads transmigration in other *inferior* forms, on this planet".

This would have dove-tailed with the preceding sentence, and would show a fact, as the Hindu *exoteric* views allow him to believe and fear the possibility of reincarnation - human and animal in turn by jumps, from man to beast and even a plant - and *vice versa*, whereas *esoteric* philosophy teaches that nature never proceeded backward in her evolutionary progress, once that man has evolved from every kind of lower forms - the mineral, vegetable, and animal kingdoms - into the human form, he can never become an animal except morally, hence - *metaphorically*. Human incarnation is a cyclic necessity, and law; and no Hindu dreads it - however much he may deplore the necessity. And this law and the periodical recurrence of man's rebirth is shown on the same page (346) and in the same unbroken paragraph, where it is closed by saying that

"But there is a way to avoid it. Buddha taught it in his doctrine of poverty, restriction of the senses, perfect indifference to the objects of this earthly vale of tears, freedom from passion, and frequent intercommunication with the Atma - soul-contemplation. *The cause of reincarnation is ignorance* ["The cause of reincarnation is ignorance" - therefore there is "reincarnation" once the writer explained the causes of it.] *of our senses, and the idea that there is any reality in the world, anything except abstract existence.* From the organs of sense comes the 'hallucination' we call contact; 'from contact, desire; from desire sensation (which also is a deception of our body), from sensation, the cleaving to existing bodies; from this cleaving, reproduction; and from reproduction, disease, decay, and death.'"

This ought to settle the question and show there must have been some carelessly unnoticed mistake and if this is not sufficient, there is something else to demonstrate it, for it is further on:

"Thus, like the revolutions of a wheel, *there is a regular succession of death and birth*, the moral cause of which is the cleaving to existing objects, while the instrumental cause is *Karma*, (the power which controls the universe, prompting it to activity), merit and demerit. It is therefore the great desire of all beings who would be *released from the sorrows of successive birth*, to seek the destruction of the moral cause, the cleaving to existing objects, or evil desire".

"They in whom evil desire is entirely destroyed are called *Arhats*. Freedom from evil desire insures the possession of a *miraculous* power. At his death, the Arhat is never reincarnated; he invariably attains nirvana - a word, by the by, falsely interpreted by the Christian scholar and skeptical commentators. Nirvana is the world of *cause*, in which all deceptive effects or delusions of our senses disappear. Nirvana is the highest attainable sphere. The *pitris* (the pre-Adamic spirits) are considered as reincarnated by the Buddhist philosopher, though in a degree far superior to that of the man of earth. Do they not die in their turn ? Do not their astral bodies suffer and rejoice, and feel the same curse of illusionary feelings as when embodied?"

And just after this we are again made to say of Buddha and his doctrine of "Merit and Demerit, or Karma:

> "But this *former life* believed in by the Buddhists, is not a life on *this planet* for, more than any other people, the Buddhistical philosopher appreciated the great doctrine of cycles."

Correct "life on this planet" by "life in the same cycle," and you will have the correct reading: for what would have appreciation of " the great doctrine of cycles " to do with Buddha's philosophy, had the great sage believed in but one short life on this Earth and in the same cycle. But to return to the real theory of reincarnation as in the esoteric teaching and its unlucky rendering in *Isis*.

Thus, what was really meant therein, was that, the principle which *does not reincarnate* - save the exceptions pointed out - is the false personality, the illusive human Entity defined and individualized; during this short life of ours, under some specific form and name; but that which *does* and has to reincarnate *nolens volens* under the unflinching, stern rule of Karmic law - is the real Ego. This confusion of the real immortal Ego in man, with the false and ephemeral *personalities* it inhabits during its Manvantaric progress, lies at the root of every such misunderstanding. Now what is the one, and what is the other ? The first group is -

1. The immortal Spirit - sexless, formless (arupa) an emanation from the One Universal Breath.

2. Its Vehicle - the *divine* Soul - called the " Immortal Ego," the " Divine Monad" etc., etc., which by accretions from *Manas* in which burns the ever-existing *Jiv* -the undying spark -adds to itself at the close of each incarnation the essence of that individuality *that was*, the aroma of the culled flower that is no more.

What is the *false* personality? It is that bundle of desires, aspirations, affection, and hatred, in short of *action*, manifested by a human being on this earth during one incarnation and under the form of one personality.[A proof how our Theosophical teachings have taken root in every class of Society and oven in English literature may be seen by reading Mr. Norman Pearson's article " Before Birth" in the *Nineteenth Century* for August, 1886. Therein, Theosophical ideas and teachings are speculated upon without acknowledgment or the smallest reference to Theosophy, and among others, we see with regard to the author's theories on the *Ego*, the following: " How much of the *individual personality* is supposed to go to heaven or hell? Does the whole of the mental equipment, good and bad, noble qualities and unholy passions, follow the soul to its hereafter ? surely not. But if not, and something has to be stripped off, how and when are we to draw the line? If, on the other hand, the Soul is something distinct from all our mental equipment, except the sense of self, are we not confronted by the incomprehensible notion of a personality without any attributes?

To this query the author answers as any true Theosophist would: " The difficulties of the question really spring from a misconception of the true nature of these attributes. The components of our mental equipment - appetites, aversions, feelings, tastes and qualities generally - are not absolute but relative existences. Hunger and thirst for instance are states of consciousness which arise in response to the stimuli of physical necessities. They are not inherent elements of the soul and *will disappear* or become modified, etc." (pp. 356 and 357). In other words, the Theosophical doctrine is adopted, Atma and Buddhi having culled off the *Manas* the aroma of the personality or *human soul* - go into Devachan; while the lower principles, the astral *simulacrum* or false personality, void of its Divine monad or spirit will remain in the *Kama-loka* - the "Summerland".] Certainly it is not all *this* which as a fact for us, the deluded, material, and materially thinking lot - is Mr. So and So, or Mrs. Somebody else - that remains immortal, or is ever reborn.

All that bundle of *Egotism* that apparent and evanescent "/" disappears after death, as the costume of the part he played disappears from the actor's body, after he leaves the theatre and goes to bed. That actor rebecomes the same " John Smith " or Gray, he was from his birth and is no longer the Othello or Hamlet that he had represented for a few hours. Nothing remains now of that "bundle" to go to the next incarnation, except *the seed for future Karma* that *Manas* may have united to its immortal group, to form with it - the disembodied *Higher Self* in " Devachan ". As to the four lower principles, that which becomes of them is found in most classics, from which we mean to quote at length for our defence. The doctrine of the *perisprit* the "false personality/' or the remains of the deceased under their astral form-fading out to disappear in time, is terribly distasteful to the spiritualists, who insist upon confusing the temporary with the immortal Ego.

Unfortunately for them and happily for us, it is not the modern Occultists who have invented the doctrine. They are on their defence. And they prove what they say, *i.e.*, that no *personality* has ever yet been " reincarnated " " on the same planet" (*our earth,* this once there is *no* mistake), save in the three exceptional cases above cited. Adding to these a fourth case, *which is the deliberate, conscious act of adeptship*; and that such an *astral* body belongs *neither to the body nor the soul* still less to the immortal spirit of man, the following is brought forward and proofs cited.

Before one brings out on the strength of undeniable manifestations, theories as to what produces them and claims at once on *prima facie* evidence that it is the *spirits* of the departed mortals that revisit us, it behooves one first to study what antiquity has declared on the subject. Ghosts and apparitions, materialized and semi-material " Spirits" have not originated with Allan Kardec, nor at Rochester. If those beings whose invariable habit is to give themselves out for *souls* and the phantoms of the dead, choose to do so and succeed, it is only because the cautious philosophy , of old is now replaced by an *a priori* conceit, and unproven assumptions. The first question is to be settled - "Have spirits any kind of substance to clothe themselves with?" *Answer.* That which is now called *perisprit* in France, and a " materialized Form" in England and America, was called in days of old *peri-psyche*, and *peri-nous* hence was well known to the old Greeks. Have they a body whether gaseous, fluidic, etherial, material, or semi- material ? No; we say this on the authority of the occult teachings the world over. For with the Hindus *atma* or *spirit* is Arupa (bodiless), and with the Greeks also. Even in the Roman Catholic Church the angels of Light as those of Darkness *are absolutely incorporeal:* " *meri spiritus, omnes corporis expertes*" and in the words of the Secret Doctrine, *primordial.* Emanations of the undifferentiated Principle, the Dhyan Chohans of the one (First) category or Pure Spiritual Essence, are formed of the *Spirit of the one Element*; the second category of the second Emanation of the Soul of the Elements ; the third have a " *mind body* " to which they are not subject, but that they can assume and govern as a body, subject *to them*, pliant to their will in form and substance. Parting from this (third) category, they (the spirits, angels, Devas or Dhyan Chohans) have Bodies the *first rupa* group of which is composed of one element *Ether* the second, of two - Ether and fire ; the third, of three - Ether, fire, and water; the fourth, of four - Ether, air, fire, and water. Then comes man, who, besides the four elements, has the fifth that predominates in him - Earth therefore he suffers. Of the Angels, as said by St. Augustine and Peter Lombard, their bodies are made *to act* not to suffer. It is earth and water, *humor et humus* that gives an aptitude for suffering and passivity, *ad patientiam*, and *Ether* and *Fire* for action. The spirits or human *monads*, belonging to the first, or undifferentiated essence are thus incorporeal; but their third principle (or the human Fifth - *Manas*) can in conjunction with its vehicle become *Kama rupa* and *Mayavi rupa* - body of desire or " illusion body ". After death, the best, noblest, purest qualities of Manas or the *human* soul ascending along with the divine Monad into "Devachan whence no one emerges from or returns, except at the time of reincarnation - what is that then which appears under the double mask of the spiritual *Ego* or soul of the departed individual ? *The Kama rupa element with the help of elementals.* For we are taught that those spiritual beings that can assume a form at will and appear, *i.e.*, make themselves objective and even tangible - are the angels alone (the Dhyan Chohans) and the *nirmanakaya*, [*Nirmanakaya* is the name given to the astral forms (*in their completeness*) of adepts, who have progressed too high on the *path of knowledge* and absolute truth, to go Into the state of Devachan; and have on the other hand, deliberately refused the bliss of nirvana, in order to help Humanity by invisibly guiding and helping on the same path of progress elect men, But these *astrals* are not empty shells, but complete monads made up of the 3rd, 4th, 5th, 6th and 7th principles. There is another order of *nirmanakaya*, however, of which much will be said in the *Secret Doctrine*. - H. P. B.] of the adepts, whose spirits are clothed in sublime matter. The astral bodies - the *remnants* and *dregs* of a mortal being which has been disembodied, when they do appear, are not the individuals they claim to be, but only their simulachres. And such was the belief of the whole of antiquity, from Homer to Swedenborg ; from the *third* race down to our own day.

More than one devoted spiritualist has hitherto quoted Paul as corroborating his claims that spirits do and can appear. " There is a natural and there is a spiritual body," etc., etc. (*I, Cor.*, xv, 44); but one has only to study closer the verses preceding and following the one quoted, to perceive that what St. Paul meant was quite different from the sense claimed for it. Surely there is a *spiritual* body, but it is not identical with the *astral* form contained in the " natural " man. The " spiritual " is formed only by our individuality *unclothed* and *transformed after death*; for the apostle takes care to explain in Verses 51 and 52, "*Immut abitnur sed non omnes*" Behold, I tell you a *mystery*; we shall *not all sleep* but we *shall all be changed*. This corruptible must put on incorruption and this mortal must put on immortality.

But this is no proof except for the Christians. Let us see what the old Egyptians and the Neo-Platonists - *both " theurgists " par excellence*, thought on the subject. They divided man into three principal groups subdivided into principles as we do: pure immortal spirit, the " Spectral Soul" (*a luminous phantom*) and the gross material body. Apart from the latter which was considered as the terrestrial shell, these groups were divided into six principles: (1) *Kha* "vital body"; (2) *Khaba* "astral form," or shadow ; (3) *Khou* "animal soul" ; (4) *Akh* "terrestrial intelligence"; (5) *Sa* "the divine soul" (*or Budddhi*); and (6) *Sah* or mummy, the functions of which began after death. *Osiris* was the highest uncreated spirit, for it was, in one sense a generic name, every man becoming after his translation *Osirified, i.e.,* absorbed into Osiris - *Sun* or into the glorious divine state. It was Khou with the lower portions of Akh or Kama rupa with the addition of the dregs of Manas remaining all behind in the astral light of our atmosphere - that formed the counterparts of the terrible and so much dreaded bhoot of the Hindus (our ' elementaries "). This is seen in the rendering made of the so-called " Harris, Papyrus on magic" (*papyrus magique,* translated by Chabas), who calls them Kouey or Khou, and explains that according to the hieroglyphics they were called Khou or the " revivified dead," the " resurrected shadows" [Placing those parallel with the division in' esoteric teaching we see that (1) *Osiris* is Atma; (2) *Sa* is Buddhi; (3) *Akh* is Manas; (4) *Khou* is Kama- rupa, the seat of the terrestrial desires; (5) *Khaba* is Lingha Sarira; (6) *Kha* is Pranatma (vital principle); (7) *Sah* is mummy or body.]

When it was said of a person that he *had a Khou.* it meant that he was possessed by a "Spirit". There were two kinds of *Khous* - the justified ones - who after living for a short time a *second life* (*nam onh*) faded out, disappeared ; and those *Khous* who were condemned to wandering without rest in darkness after *dying for a second time - mut, em, nam* - and who were called the H'ou - métre ("second time dead") which did not prevent them from clinging to a vicarious life after the manner of Vampires. How dreaded they were is explained in our Appendices on Egyptian Magic and " Chinese Spirits" (*Secret Doctrine*}. They were exorcised by Egyptian priests as the evil spirit is exorcised by the Roman Catholic curé; or again the Chinese *houen,* identical with the *Khou* and the " Elementary," as also with the *lares* or *larvae* - a word derived from the former by Festus, the grammarian; who explains that they were " *the shadows of the dead who gave no rest in the house they were in* either to the Masters or the servants". These creatures when evoked during theurgic, and especially *necromantic* rites, were regarded, and are regarded so still, in China - as neither the Spirit, nor any thing belonging to the deceased personality they represented, but simply, as his reflection - *simmulacrum*.

"The human soul says Apuleius, " is an *immortal God*" (Buddhi) which nevertheless has his beginning. When death rids it (the Soul), from its earthly corporeal organism, it is called *lemure*. There are among the latter not a few who are beneficent, and which become the gods or demons of the family, *i.e.*, its domestic gods: - in which case they are called *lares*. But they are vilified and spoken of as *larvae* when sentenced by fate to wander about, they spread around them evil and plagues (*Inane terriculamentum, ceterum noxium malis*;) or if their real nature is doubtful they are referred to as simply *manes* (Apuleius, see - *Du Dieu de Socrate*, pages. 143 - 145. Edit. Niz.) Listen to Yamblichus, Proclus, Porphyry, Psellus, and to dozens of other writers on these mystic subjects.

The Magi of Chaldea believed and *taught that the celestial or divine soul* would participate in the bliss of eternal light, while the animal or *sensuous* soul would, if good, rapidly dissolve, and if wicked, go on wandering about in the Earth's sphere. In this case, " it (the soul) assumes at times the forms of various human phantoms and even those of animals ". The same was said of the *Eidólon* of the Greeks, and of their *Nephesh* by the Rabbins: (see *Sciences Occultes*, Count de Resie, V, 11). All the *Illuminati* of the middle ages tell us of our *astral Soul*, the reflection of the dead or his *spectre*. At *Natal* death (birth) the pure spirit remains attached to the *intermediate* and *luminous* body but as soon as its lower form (the physical body) is dead, the former ascends heavenward, and the latter descends into the nether worlds, or the *Kama loka*.

Homer shows us the body of Patroclus - the true image of the terrestrial body lying killed by Hector - rising in its spiritual form, and Lucretius shows old Ennius representing Homer himself, shedding bitter tears, amidst the *shadows and the human simulachres* on the shores of Acherusia *where live neither our bodies nor our souls*, but only our images.

> "*Esse Acherusia templa,*
> *Quo neque permanent animoe, neque corpora nostra,*
> *Sed queedam simulacra*

Virgil called it *imago* "image" and in the Odyssey (I, xi), the author refers to it as the type, the model, and at the same time the copy of the body ; since Telamachus will not recognize Ulyssus and seeks to drive him off by saying - " No thou art not my father; thou art a demon trying to seduce me!" (*Odys* I, xvi, v. 194.) "Latins do not lack significant proper names to designate the varieties of their demons ; and thus they called them in turn, *lares, lemures, geni and manes*." Cicero, in translating Plato's *Timaeus* translates the word *daimones* by *lares*;and Festus the grammarian, explains that the inferior or lower gods were the *souls of men,* making a difference between the two as Homer did, and between *anima bruta*, and *anima divina* (animal and divine souls). Plutarch (in *proble. Rom.*) makes the lares preside and inhabit the (haunted) houses, and calls them, cruel, exacting, inquisitive, etc., etc. Festus thinks that there are good and bad ones among the lares. For he calls them at one time *proestites* as they gave occasionally, and watched over things care-fully (*direct apports*), and at another - *hostilens*? "[Because they drove the enemies away.] However it may be," says in his queer old French, Leloyer, " they are no better than our devils, who, if they do appear helping sometimes men, and presenting them with property, it is only to hurt them the better and the more later on. *Lemures* are also devils and *larvae* for they appear at night in various human and animal forms, but still more frequently with features that *they borrow from dead men.*" (*Livre des Spectres*, V. iv, pp. 15 and 16.)

After this little honour rendered to his Christian preconceptions, that see Satan everywhere, Leloyer speaks like an Occultist, and a very erudite one too.

"It is quite certain that the *genii* and none other had mission to watch over every newly born man, and that they were called *genii*, as says Censorius, because they had in their charge our race, and not only they *presided* over every mortal being but over whole generations and tribes, being the *genii of the people.*"

The idea of guardian angels of men, races, localities, cities, and nations, was taken by the Roman Catholics from the pre-Christian occultists and pagans. Symmachus (Epistol, I, X) writes : " As souls are given to those who are born, so *genii* are distributed to the nations. Every city had its protecting genius, to whom the people sacrificed." There is more than one inscription found that reads: *Genio civitates* - " to the genius of the city."

Only the ancient profane, never seemed sure any more than the modern whether an apparition was the *eidolon* of a relative or the genius of the locality. Enneus while celebrating the anniversary of the name of his father Anchises, seeing a serpent crawling on his tomb knew not whether that was the *genius* of his father or the genius of the place. (Virgil). " The *manes* [From manus - "good," an , as Festus explains.] were numbered and divided between good and bad; those that were *sinister*, and that Virgil calls *numina larva*, were appeased by sacrifices that they should commit no mischief, such as sending bad dreams to those who despised them, etc.

Tibullus shows by his line:

Ne tibi neglecti militant insomnia manes. (Eleg., i, II.)

"Pagans thought that the *lower Souls* were transformed after death into *diabolical aerial* spirits." (Leloyer, page 22.)

The term *Eteroprosopos* when divided into its several compound words will yield a whole sentence, " an other than I under the features of my person ".

It is to this terrestrial principle, the *eidolon*, the *larva*, the *bhoot* - call it by whatever name - that reincarnation was refused in *Isis* [Page 12, Volume I, of *Isis Unveiled*, belief in reincarnation is asserted from the very beginning, as forming part and parcel of universal beliefs. " Metempsychosis " (or transmigration of souls) and reincarnation being after all the same thing.]

The doctrines of Theosophy are simply the faithful echoes of Antiquity. Man is a *Unity* only at his origin and at his end. All the Spirits, all the Souls, gods, and demons emanate from and have for their root- principle the Soul of the Universe - says Porphyry (*De Sacrifice*). Not a Philosopher of any notoriety who did not believe (1) in reincarnation (metempsychosis), (2) in the plurality of principles in man, or that man had *two Souls* of separate and quite different nature ; one perishable, the *Astral Soul*, the other incorruptible and immortal; and (3) that the former was not the man whom it represented - "neither his spirit nor his body, but his *reflection*, at best ". This was taught by Brahmins, Buddhists, Hebrews, Greeks, Egyptians, and Chaldeans; by the post-diluvian heirs of the prediluvian Wisdom, by Pythagoras and Socrates, Clemens Alexandrinus, Synesius, and Origen, the oldest Greek poets as much as the Gnostics, whom Gibbon shows as the most refined, learned and enlightened men of all ages (see " *Decline and Fall*," etc.). But the rabble was the same in every age : superstitious, self-opinionated, materializing every most spiritual and noblest idealistic conception and dragging it down to its own low level, and - ever adverse to philosophy.

But all this does not interfere with the fact, that our "fifth Race" man, analyzed esoterically as a septenary creature, was ever *exoterically* recognized as mundane, sub-mundane, terrestrial and supra mundane, Ovid graphically describing him as –

Bis duo sunt hominis ; manes, caro, spiritus, umbra
Quatuor ista loca bis duo suscipiunt.
Terra tegit carnem, tumulum circumvolat umbra,
Orus habet manes, epiritus astra petit.

Ostende, Oct., 1886.

AN IMPORTANT CORRECTION [From The Path, January, 1887.]

To ALL THE READERS OF *The Path*,

In the November number of *The Path*, in my article " Theories About Reincarnation and Spirits," the entire batch of elaborate arguments is upset and made to fall flat owing to the mistake of either copyist or printer. On page 235, the last paragraph is made to begin . with these words : " Therefore the *reincarnating* principles are left behind in *Kama-loka*, etc.," whereas it ought to read, "Therefore the Non- *reincarnating* principles (the false personality) are left behind in Kama-loka, etc. a statement fully corroborated by what follows, since it is stated that those principles fade out and *disappear*.

There seems to be some fatality attending this question. The spiritualists will not fail to see in it the guiding hand of their dear departed ones from " Summerland " ; and I am inclined to share that belief with them in so far that there must be some mischievous spook between me and the printing of my articles. Unless immediately corrected and attention drawn to it, this error is one which is sure to be quoted some day against me and called a *contradiction.*

Yours truly,

H. P. BLAVATSKY.

November 20th 1886.

Note. - The MS. for the article referred to was written out by someone for Mme. Blavatsky and forwarded to us as it was printed, and it is quite evident that the error was the copyist's, and not ours nor Madame's ; besides that, the remainder of the paragraph clearly shows a mistake. We did not feel justified in making such an important change on our own responsibility, but are now glad to have the author do it herself. Other minor errors probably also can be found in consequence of the peculiar writing of the amanuensis, but they are very trivial in their nature. - Editor. *[The Path]*

ON THE MYSTERIES OF REINCARNATION

Periodical Rebirths

Q. You mean, then, that we have all lived on earth before, in many past incarnations, and shall go on so living?

A. I do. The life cycle, or rather the cycle of conscious life, begins with the separation of the mortal animal-man into sexes, and will end with the close of the last generation of men, in the seventh round and seventh race of mankind. Considering we are only in the fourth round and fifth race, its duration is more easily imagined than expressed.

Q. And we keep on incarnating in new personalities all the time?

A. Most assuredly so; because this life cycle or period of incarnation may be best compared to human life. As each such life is composed of days of activity separated by nights of sleep or of inaction, so, in the incarnation cycle, an active life is followed by a Devachanic rest.

Q. And it is this succession of births that is generally defined as reincarnation?

A. Just so. It is only through these births that the perpetual progress of the countless millions of Egos toward final perfection and final rest (as long as was the period of activity) can be achieved.

Q. And what is it that regulates the duration, or special qualities of these incarnations?

A. Karma, the universal law of retributive justice.

Q. Is it an intelligent law?

A. For the Materialist, who calls the law of periodicity which regulates the marshaling of the several bodies, and all the other laws in nature, blind forces and mechanical laws, no doubt Karma would be a law of chance and no more. For us, no adjective or qualification could describe that which is impersonal and no entity, but a universal operative law. If you question me about the causative intelligence in it, I must answer you I do not know. But if you ask me to define its effects and tell you what these are in our belief, I may say that the experience of thousands of ages has shown us that they are absolute and unerring equity, wisdom, and intelligence. For Karma in its effects is an unfailing redresser of human injustice, and of all the failures of nature; a stern adjuster of wrongs; a retributive law which rewards and punishes with equal impartiality. It is, in the strictest sense, "no respecter of persons," though, on the other hand, it can neither be propitiated, nor turned aside by prayer. This is a belief common to Hindus and Buddhists, who both believe in Karma.

Q. In this Christian dogmas contradict both, and I doubt whether any Christian will accept the teaching.

A. No; and Inman gave the reason for it many years ago. As he puts it, while
… the Christians will accept any nonsense, if promulgated by the Church as a matter of faith … the Buddhists hold that nothing which is contradicted by sound reason can be a true doctrine of Buddha.

They do not believe in any pardon for their sins, except after an adequate and just punishment for each evil deed or thought in a future incarnation, and a proportionate compensation to the parties injured.

Q. Where is it so stated?

A. In most of their sacred works. Consider the following Theosophical tenet:

Buddhists believe that every act, word, or thought has its consequence, which will appear sooner or later in the present or in the future state. Evil acts will produce evil consequences, good acts will produce good consequences: prosperity in this world, or birth in heaven (Devachan) ... in the future state.

Q. Christians believe the same thing, don't they?

A. Oh, no; they believe in the pardon and the remission of all sins. They are promised that if they only believe in the blood of Christ (an innocent victim!), in the blood offered by Him for the expiation of the sins of the whole of mankind, it will atone for every mortal sin. And we believe neither in vicarious atonement, nor in the possibility of the remission of the smallest sin by any god, not even by a "personal Absolute" or "Infinite," if such a thing could have any existence. What we believe in, is strict and impartial justice. Our idea of the unknown Universal Deity, represented by Karma, is that it is a Power which cannot fail, and can, therefore, have neither wrath nor mercy, only absolute Equity, which leaves every cause, great or small, to work out its inevitable effects. The saying of Jesus: "With what measure you mete it shall be measured to you again," neither by expression nor implication points to any hope of future mercy or salvation by proxy. This is why, recognizing as we do in our philosophy the justice of this statement, we cannot recommend too strongly mercy, charity, and forgiveness of mutual offenses. Resist not evil, and render good for evil, are Buddhist precepts, and were first preached in view of the implacability of Karmic law. For man to take the law into his own hands is anyhow a sacrilegious presumption. Human Law may use restrictive not punitive measures; but a man who, believing in Karma, still revenges himself and refuses to forgive every injury, thereby rendering good for evil, is a criminal and only hurts himself. As Karma is sure to punish the man who wronged him, by seeking to inflict an additional punishment on his enemy, he, who instead of leaving that punishment to the great Law adds to it his own mite, only begets thereby a cause for the future reward of his own enemy and a future punishment for himself. The unfailing Regulator affects in each incarnation the quality of its successor; and the sum of the merit or demerit in preceding ones determines it.

Q. Are we then to infer a man's past from his present?

A. Only so far as to believe that his present life is what it justly should be, to atone for the sins of the past life. Of course-seers and great adepts excepted-we cannot as average mortals know what those sins were. From our paucity of data, it is impossible for us even to determine what an old man's youth must have been; neither can we, for like reasons, draw final conclusions merely from what we see in the life of some man, as to what his past life may have been.

What is Karma?

Q. But what is Karma?

A. As I have said, we consider it as the Ultimate Law of the Universe, the source, origin, and fount of all other laws which exist throughout Nature. Karma is the unerring law which adjusts effect to cause, on the physical, mental, and spiritual planes of being. As no cause remains without its due effect from greatest to least, from a cosmic disturbance down to the movement of your hand, and as like produces like, Karma is that unseen and unknown law which adjusts wisely, intelligently, and equitably each effect to its cause, tracing the latter back to its producer. Though itself unknowable, its action is perceivable.

Q. Then it is the "Absolute," the "Unknowable" again, and is not of much value as an explanation of the problems of life?

A. On the contrary. For, though we do not know what Karma is per se, and in its essence, we do know how it works, and we can define and describe its mode of action with accuracy. We only do not know its ultimate Cause, just as modern philosophy universally admits that the ultimate Cause of anything is "unknowable."

Q. And what has Theosophy to say in regard to the solution of the more practical needs of humanity? What is the explanation which it offers in reference to the awful suffering and dire necessity prevalent among the so-called "lower classes."

A. To be pointed, according to our teaching all these great social evils, the distinction of classes in Society, and of the sexes in the affairs of life, the unequal distribution of capital and of labor-all are due to what we tersely but truly denominate Karma.

Q. But, surely, all these evils which seem to fall upon the masses somewhat indiscriminately are not actual merited and individual Karma?

A. No, they cannot be so strictly defined in their effects as to show that each individual environment, and the particular conditions of life in which each person finds himself, are nothing more than the retributive Karma which the individual generated in a previous life. We must not lose sight of the fact that every atom is subject to the general law governing the whole body to which it belongs, and here we come upon the wider track of the Karmic law. Do you not perceive that the aggregate of individual Karma becomes that of the nation to which those individuals belong, and further, that the sumtotal of National Karma is that of the World? The evils that you speak of are not peculiar to the individual or even to the Nation, they are more or less universal; and it is upon this broad line of Human interdependence that the law of Karma finds its legitimate and equable issue.

Q. Do I, then, understand that the law of Karma is not necessarily an individual law?

A. That is just what I mean. It is impossible that Karma could readjust the balance of power in the world's life and progress, unless it had a broad and general line of action. It is held as a truth among Theosophists that the interdependence of Humanity is the cause of what is called Distributive Karma, and it is this law which affords the solution to the great question of collective suffering and its relief. It is an occult law, moreover, that no man can rise superior to his individual failings, without lifting, be it ever so little, the whole body of which he is an integral part. In the same way, no one can sin, nor suffer the effects of sin, alone. In reality, there is no such thing as "Separateness"; and the nearest approach to that selfish state, which the laws of life permit, is in the intent or motive.

Q. And are there no means by which the distributive or national Karma might be concentrated or collected, so to speak, and brought to its natural and legitimate fulfillment without all this protracted suffering?

A. As a general rule, and within certain limits which define the age to which we belong, the law of Karma cannot be hastened or retarded in its fulfillment. But of this I am certain, the point of possibility in either of these directions has never yet been touched. Listen to the following recital of one phase of national suffering, and then ask yourself whether, admitting the working power of individual, relative, and distributive Karma, these evils are not capable of extensive modification and general relief. What I am about to read to you is from the pen of a National Savior, one who, having overcome Self, and being free to choose, has elected to serve Humanity, in bearing at least as much as a woman's shoulders can possibly bear of National Karma. This is what she says:

> Yes, Nature always does speak, don't you think? Only sometimes we make so much noise that we drown her voice. That is why it is so restful to go out of the town and nestle awhile in the Mother's arms. I am thinking of the evening on Hampstead Heath when we watched the sun go down; but oh! upon what suffering and misery that sun had set! A lady brought me yesterday a big hamper of wild flowers. I thought some of my East-end family had a better right to it than I, and so I took it down to a very poor school in Whitechapel this morning. You should have seen the pallid little faces brighten! Thence I went to pay for some dinners at a little cookshop for some children. It was in a back street, narrow, full of jostling people; stench indescribable, from fish, meat, and other food, all reeking in a sun that, in Whitechapel,

festers instead of purifying. The cookshop was the quintessence of all the smells. Indescribable meat-pies at 1d., loathsome lumps of 'food' and swarms of flies, a very altar of Beelzebub! All about, babies on the prowl for scraps, one, with the face of an angel, gathering up cherrystones as a light and nutritious form of diet. I came westward with every nerve shuddering and jarred, wondering whether anything can be done with some parts of London save swallowing them up in an earthquake and starting their inhabitants afresh, after a plunge into some purifying Lethe, out of which not a memory might emerge! And then I thought of Hampstead Heath, and-pondered. If by any sacrifice one could win the power to save these people, the cost would not be worth counting; but, you see, they must be changed-and how can that be wrought? In the condition they now are, they would not profit by any environment in which they might be placed; and yet, in their present surroundings they must continue to putrefy. It breaks my heart, this endless, hopeless misery, and the brutish degradation that is at once its outgrowth and its root. It is like the banyan tree; every branch roots itself and sends out new shoots. What a difference between these feelings and the peaceful scene at Hampstead! and yet we, who are the brothers and sisters of these poor creatures, have only a right to use Hampstead Heaths to gain strength to save Whitechapels.

Q. That is a sad but beautiful letter, and I think it presents with painful conspicuity the terrible workings of what you have called "Relative and Distributive Karma." But alas! there seems no immediate hope of any relief short of an earthquake, or some such general engulfment!

A. What right have we to think so while one-half of humanity is in a position to effect an immediate relief of the privations which are suffered by their fellows? When every individual has contributed to the general good what he can of money, of labor, and of ennobling thought, then, and only then, will the balance of National Karma be struck, and until then we have no right nor any reasons for saying that there is more life on the earth than Nature can support. It is reserved for the heroic souls, the Saviors of our Race and Nation, to find out the cause of this unequal pressure of retributive Karma, and by a supreme effort to readjust the balance of power, and save the people from a moral engulfment a thousand times more disastrous and more permanently evil than the like physical catastrophe, in which you seem to see the only possible outlet for this accumulated misery.

Q. Well, then, tell me generally how you describe this law of Karma?

A. We describe Karma as that Law of readjustment which ever tends to restore disturbed equilibrium in the physical, and broken harmony in the moral world. We say that Karma does not act in this or that particular way always; but that it always does act so as to restore Harmony and preserve the balance of equilibrium, in virtue of which the Universe exists.

Q. Give me an illustration.

A. Later on I will give you a full illustration. Think now of a pond. A stone falls into the water and creates disturbing waves. These waves oscillate backwards and forwards till at last, owing to the operation of what physicists call the law of the dissipation of energy, they are brought to rest, and the water returns to its condition of calm tranquility. Similarly all action, on every plane, produces disturbance in the balanced harmony of the Universe, and the vibrations so produced will continue to roll backwards and forwards, if its area is limited, till equilibrium is restored. But since each such disturbance starts from some particular point, it is clear that equilibrium and harmony can only be restored by the reconverging to that same point of all the forces which were set in motion from it. And here you have proof that the consequences of a man's deeds, thoughts, etc. must all react upon himself with the same force with which they were set in motion.

Q. But I see nothing of a moral character about this law. It looks to me like the simple physical law that action and reaction are equal and opposite.

A. I am not surprised to hear you say that. Europeans have got so much into the ingrained habit of considering right and wrong, good and evil, as matters of an arbitrary code of law laid down either by men, or imposed upon them by a Personal God. We Theosophists, however, say that "Good" and "Harmony," and "Evil" and "Disharmony," are synonymous. Further we maintain that all pain and suffering are results of want of Harmony, and that the one terrible and only cause of the disturbance of Harmony is selfishness in some form or another. Hence Karma gives back to every man the actual consequences of his own actions, without any regard to their moral character; but since he receives his due for all, it is obvious that he will be made to atone for all sufferings which he has caused, just as he will reap in joy and gladness the fruits of all the happiness and harmony he had helped to produce. I can do no better than quote for your benefit certain passages from books and articles written by our Theosophists-those who have a correct idea of Karma.

Q. I wish you would, as your literature seers to be very sparing on this subject?

A. Because it is the most difficult of all our tenets. Some short time ago there appeared the following objection from a Christian pen:

> Granting that the teaching in regard to Theosophy is correct, and that "man must be his own savior, must overcome self and conquer the evil that is in his dual nature, to obtain the emancipation of his soul," what is man to do after he has been awakened and converted to a certain extent from evil or wickedness? How is he to get emancipation, or pardon, or the blotting out of the evil or wickedness he has already done?

To this Mr. J.H. Conelly replies very pertinently that no one can hope to "make the theosophical engine run on the theological track." As he has it:

> The possibility of shirking individual responsibility is not among the concepts of Theosophy. In this faith there is no such thing as pardoning, or "blotting out of evil or wickedness already done," otherwise than by the adequate punishment therefore of the wrong-doer and the restoration of the harmony in the universe that had been disturbed by his wrongful act. The evil has been his own, and while others must suffer its consequences, atonement can be made by nobody but himself.
>
> The condition contemplated ... in which a man shall have been "awakened and converted to a certain extent from evil or wickedness," is that in which a man shall have realized that

his deeds are evil and deserving of punishment. In that realization a sense of personal responsibility is inevitable, and just in proportion to the extent of his awakening or "converting" must be the sense of that awful responsibility. While it is strong upon him is the time when he is urged to accept the doctrine of vicarious atonement.

He is told that he must also repent, but nothing is easier than that. It is an amiable weakness of human nature that we are quite prone to regret the evil we have done when our attention is called, and we have either suffered from it ourselves or enjoyed its fruits. Possibly, close analysis of the feeling would show us that thing which we regret is rather the necessity that seemed to require the evil as a means of attainment of our selfish ends than the evil itself.

Attractive as this prospect of casting our burden of sins "at the foot of the cross" may be to the ordinary mind, it does not commend itself to the Theosophic student. He does not apprehend why the sinner by attaining knowledge of his evil can thereby merit any pardon for or the blotting out of his past wickedness; or why repentance and future right living entitle him to a suspension in his favor of the universal law of relation between cause and effect. The results of his evil deeds continue to exist; the suffering caused to others by his wickedness is not blotted out. The Theosophical student takes the result of wickedness upon the innocent into his problem. He considers not only the guilty person, but his victims.

Evil is an infraction of the laws of harmony governing the universe, and the penalty thereof must fall upon the violator of that law himself. Christ uttered the warning, "Sin no more, lest a worse thing come upon thee," and St. Paul said, "Work out your own salvation. Whatsoever a man soweth, that shall he also reap." That, by the way, is a fine metaphoric rendering of the sentence of the Pur as far antedating him-that "every man reaps the consequences of his own acts."

This is the principle of the law of Karma which is taught by Theosophy. Sinnett, in his Esoteric Buddhism, rendered Karma as "the law of ethical causation." "The law of retribution," as Mme. Blavatsky translates its meaning, is better. It is the power which

> Just though mysterious, leads us on unerring
> Through ways unmarked from guilt to punishment.

But it is more. It rewards merit as unerringly and amply as it punishes demerit. It is the outcome of every act, of thought, word, and deed, and by it men mold themselves, their lives and happenings. Eastern philosophy rejects the idea of a newly created soul for every baby born. It believes in a limited number of monads, evolving and growing more and more perfect through their assimilation of many successive personalities. Those personalities are the product of Karma and it is by Karma and reincarnation that the human monad in time returns to its source-absolute deity.

E.D. Walker, in his Reincarnation, offers the following explanation:

> Briefly, the doctrine of Karma is that we have made ourselves what we are by former actions, and are building our future eternity by present actions. There is no destiny but what we

ourselves determine. There is no salvation or condemnation except what we ourselves bring about ... Because it offers no shelter for culpable actions and necessitates a sterling manliness, it is less welcome to weak natures than the easy religious tenets of vicarious atonement, intercession, forgiveness, and deathbed conversions ... In the domain of eternal justice the offense and the punishment are inseparably connected as the same event, because there is no real distinction between the action and its outcome ... It is Karma, or our old acts, that draws us back into earthly life. The spirit's abode changes according to its Karma, and this Karma forbids any long continuance in one condition, because it is always changing. So long as action is governed by material and selfish motives, just so long must the effect of that action be manifested in physical rebirths. Only the perfectly selfless man can elude the gravitation of material life. Few have attained this, but it is the goal of mankind.

And then the writer quotes from The Secret Doctrine:

> Those who believe in Karma have to believe in destiny, which, from birth to death, every man is weaving, thread by thread, around himself, as a spider does his cobweb, and this destiny is guided either by the heavenly voice of the invisible prototype outside of us, or by our more intimate astral or inner man, who is but too often the evil genius of the embodied entity called man. Both these lead on the outward man, but one of them must prevail; and from the very beginning of the invisible affray the stern and implacable law of compensation steps in and takes its course, faithfully following the fluctuations. When the last strand is woven, and man is seemingly enwrapped in the network of his own

doing, then he finds himself completely under the empire of this self-made destiny ... An Occultist or a philosopher will not speak of the goodness or cruelty of Providence; but, identifying it with Karma-Nemesis, he will teach that, nevertheless, it guards the good and watches over them in this as in future lives; and that it punishes the evil-doer-aye, even to his seventh rebirth-so long, in short, as the effect of his having thrown into perturbation even the smallest atom in the infinite world of harmony has not been finally readjusted. For the only decree of Karma-an eternal and immutable decree-is absolute harmony in the world of matter as it is in the world of spirit. It is not, therefore, Karma that rewards or punishes, but it is we who reward or punish ourselves according to whether we work with, through and along with nature, abiding by the laws on which that harmony depends, or-break them. Nor would the ways of Karma be inscrutable were men to work in union and harmony, instead of disunion and strife. For our ignorance of those ways-which one portion of mankind calls the ways of Providence, dark and intricate; while another sees in them the action of blind fatalism; and a third simple chance, with neither gods nor devils to guide them-would surely disappear if we would but attribute all these to their correct cause ... We stand bewildered before the mystery of our own making and the riddles of life that we will not solve, and then accuse the great Sphinx of devouring us. But verily there is not an accident of our lives, not a misshapen day, or a misfortune, that could not be traced back to our own doings in this or in another life ... The law of Karma is inextricably interwoven with that of reincarnation ... It is only this doctrine that can explain to us the mysterious problem of good and evil, and reconcile man to the terrible and apparent injustice of life.

Nothing but such certainty can quiet our revolted sense of justice. For, when one unacquainted with the noble doctrine looks around him and observes the inequalities of birth and fortune, of intellect and capacities; when one sees honor paid to fools and wastrels, on whom fortune has heaped her favors by mere privilege of birth, and their nearest neighbor, with all his intellect and noble virtues-far more deserving in every way-perishing for want and for lack of sympathy-when one sees all this and has to turn away, helpless to relieve the undeserved suffering, one's ears ringing and heart aching with the cries of pain around him-that blessed knowledge of Karma alone prevents him from cursing life and men as well as their supposed Creator ... This law, whether conscious or unconscious, predestines nothing and no one. It exists from and in eternity truly, for it is eternity itself; and as such, since no act can be coequal with eternity, it cannot be said to act, for it is action itself. It is not the wave which drowns the man, but the personal action of the wretch who goes deliberately and places himself under the impersonal action of the laws that govern the ocean's motion. Karma creates nothing, nor does it design. It is man who plants and creates causes, and Karmic law adjusts the effects, which adjustment is not an act but universal harmony, tending ever to resume its original position, like a bough, which, bent down too forcibly, rebounds with corresponding vigor. If it happen to dislocate the arm that tried to bend it out of its natural position, shall we say it is the bough which broke our arm or that our own folly has brought us to grief? Karma has never sought to destroy intellectual and individual liberty, like the god invented by the Monotheists. It has not involved its decrees in darkness purposely to perplex man, nor shall it punish him who dares to scrutinize its mysteries. On the contrary, he who unveils through study and meditation its intricate paths, and throws light on those dark ways, in the windings of which so many men perish owing to their ignorance of the labyrinth of life, is working for the good of his fellowmen. Karma is an absolute and eternal law in the world of manifestation; and as there can only be one Absolute, as one Eternal, ever-present Cause, believers in Karma cannot be regarded as atheists or materialists, still less as fatalists, for Karma is one with the Unknowable, of which it is an aspect, in its effects in the phenomenal world.

Another able Theosophic writer says:

Every individual is making Karma either good or bad in each action and thought of his daily round, and is at the same time working out in this life the Karma brought about by the acts and desires of the last. When we see people afflicted by congenital ailments it may be safely assumed that these ailments are the inevitable results of causes started by themselves in a previous birth. It may be argued that, as these afflictions are hereditary, they can have nothing to do with a past incarnation; but it must be remembered that the Ego, the real man, the individuality, has no spiritual origin in the parentage by which it is reembodied, but it is drawn by the affinities which its previous mode of life attracted round it into the current that carries it, when the time comes for rebirth, to the home best fitted for the development of those tendencies ... This doctrine of Karma, when properly understood, is well calculated to guide and assist those who realize its truth to a higher and better mode of life, for it must not be forgotten that not only our actions but our thoughts also are most assuredly followed by a crowd of circumstances that will influence for good or for evil our own future, and, what is still more important, the future of many of our fellow-creatures. If sins of omission and commission could in any case be only self-regarding, the fact on the sinner's Karma would be a matter of minor consequence. The effect that every thought and act through life carries with it for good or evil a corresponding influence on other members of the human family renders a strict sense of justice, morality, and unselfishness so necessary to future happiness or progress. A crime once committed, an evil thought sent out from the mind, are past recall-no amount of repentance can wipe out their results in the future. Repentance, if sincere, will deter a man from repeating errors; it cannot save him or others from the effects of those already produced, which will most unerringly overtake him either in this life or in the next rebirth.

Mr. J.H. Conelly proceeds-

> The believers in a religion based upon such doctrine are willing it should be compared with one in which man's destiny for eternity is determined by the accidents of a single, brief earthly existence, during which he is cheered by the promise that "as the tree falls so shall it lie"; in which his brightest hope, when he wakes up to a knowledge of his wickedness, is the doctrine of vicarious atonement, and in which even that is handicapped, according to the Presbyterian Confession of Faith.
>
> By the decree of God, for the manifestation of his glory, some men and angels are predestinated unto everlasting life and others foreordained to everlasting death.

These angels and men thus predestinated and foreordained are particularly and unchangeably designed; and their number is so certain and definite that it cannot be either increased or diminished ... As God hath appointed the elect unto glory ... Neither are any other redeemed by Christ effectually called, justified, adopted, sanctified, and saved, but the elect only.

The rest of mankind God was pleased, according to the unsearchable counsel of his own will, whereby he extendeth or withholdeth mercy as he pleaseth, for the glory of his sovereign power over his creatures, to pass by and to ordain them to dishonor and wrath for their sin to the praise of his glorious justice.

This is what the able defender says. Nor can we do any better than wind up the subject as he does, by a quotation from a magnificent poem. As he says:

> The exquisite beauty of Edwin Arnold's exposition of Karma in The Light of Asia tempts to its reproduction here, but it is too long for quotation in full. Here is a portion of it:
>
>> Karma-all that total of a soul
>> Which is the things it did, the thoughts it had,
>> The "self" it wove with woof of viewless time
>> Crossed on the warp invisible of acts.
>>
>> Before beginning and without an end,
>> As space eternal and as surety sure,
>> Is fixed a Power divine which moves to good,

Only its laws endure.

It will not be despised of anyone;
Who thwarts it loses, and who serves it gains;
The hidden good it pays with peace and bliss,
The hidden ill with pains.

It seeth everywhere and marketh all;
Do right-it recompenseth! Do one wrong-
The equal retribution must be made,
Though Dharma tarry long.

It knows not wrath nor pardon; utter-true,
Its measures mete, its faultless balance weighs;
Times are as naught, tomorrow it will judge
Or after many days.

Such is the law which moves to righteousness,
Which none at last can turn aside or stay;
The heart of it is love, the end of it
Is peace and consummation sweet. Obey.

And now I advise you to compare our Theosophic views upon Karma, the law of Retribution, and say whether they are not both more philosophical and just than this cruel and idiotic dogma which makes of "God" a senseless fiend; the tenet, namely, that the "elect only" will be saved, and the rest doomed to eternal perdition!

Q. Yes, I see what you mean generally; but I wish you could give some concrete example of the action of Karma?

A. That I cannot do. We can only feel sure, as I said before, that our present lives and circumstances are the direct results of our own deeds and thoughts in lives that are past. But we, who are not Seers or Initiates, cannot know anything about the details of the working of the law of Karma.

www.ingramcontent.com/pod-product-compliance
Lightning Source LLC
LaVergne TN
LVHW041501070426
835507LV00009B/731